PLAYGROUND EDUCATION

CREATED and WRITTEN by

R. TOBIAS PITTMAN

THE EDUCATIONAL PANDA

PUGSLEY PANDA

ILLUSTRATIONS by

William Chislum

EDITED by

Gloria Miles

Hello, Kayla. How was school today?
School was great! Tomorrow is going to be even better. We are going to talk about *Character*.

Hello, Pugsley and Kayla. I heard you guys talking about *Kindness*.
Tell us how important it is to be kind.

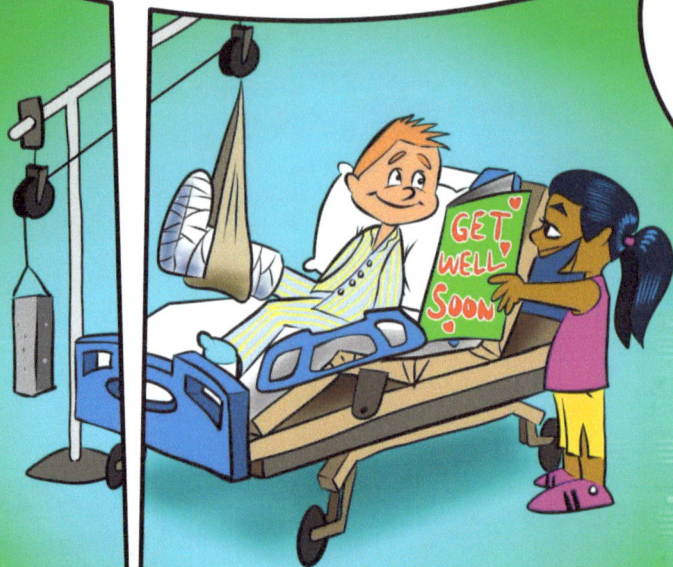

Hello, Pugsley and Kayla. Do you guys need help with politeness?
We were hoping you can help us with being Polite.

You just used one of the most polite set of words anyone can use, "Thank you".
I guess I did. My grandmother says to always say thank you.

You can politely suggest a rhyme "Close it, lock it, and put it in your pocket".
Let me try, "Close it, lock it, and put it in your pocket".
I will try that the next time I hear students talking in the library.

Well, guys,
I have to be on my way home
over to Duke Street.
May I walk with you?

Kayla, you are being so polite by saying "May I". Lets talk about more polite things to say and do as we walk home.
Goodbye, Pugsley. Here comes Jasmine, you can continue the lesson on how *Character Counts*.

"Always leave places better than how you found them, no matter what YOU have to do."

"The time is always right to do what's right"
Dr. Martin Luther King Jr.

www.ingramcontent.com/pod-product-compliance
Lightning Source LLC
Chambersburg PA
CBHW040031050426
42453CB00002B/79

9 780990 821786